Sam McCready is a well-known Irish actor, director, teacher and writer. He was born in East Belfast and attended Strand Primary and Grosvenor High School. After graduating from Stranmillis College, he taught at Fane Street Primary and Orangefield Boys' Secondary School. He was a founder member of the Lyric Players' Theatre in Derryvolgie Avenue and later a Trustee and Artistic Director of the Lyric in Ridgeway Street. He lectured at the University of Wales, 1969-78, and was Head of Drama at Stranmillis College, 1978-83. He emigrated to the United States in 1984 when he was appointed Professor of Theatre at the University of Maryland, Baltimore County. He has directed off-Broadway and appeared as an actor in a number of prestigious theatres in the US and Europe. He has received national recognition for his college theatre productions in the US and was the Artistic Director of the acclaimed summer touring production, *Shakespeare on Wheels*, 1984-93. He has directed the Drama Workshop at the Yeats International Summer School since 1998, and is in demand as an adjudicator of drama and speech festivals throughout the world. He is the author of *Lucille Lortel: A Bio-Bibliography* (1993) and *A William Butler Yeats Encyclopedia* (1997), in addition to a range of articles on world theatre. He is currently writing a history of the theatre in the north of Ireland.

COOLE LADY

COOLE LADY

The Extraordinary Story of Lady Gregory

with best wishes

SAM MCCREADY

Sam McCready.

with a preface by James Pethica

V Joan   *Cork 2014*

LAGAN PRESS
BELFAST
2006

Published by
Lagan Press
1A Bryson Street
Belfast BT5 4ES
e-mail: lagan-press@e-books.org.uk
web: www.lagan-press.org.uk

ARTS
COUNCIL
of Northern Ireland

ISBN: 1 904652 24 7
Author: Sam McCready
Title: Coole Lady
2005

First published 2005, reprinted 2006

Cover: Joan McCready as Lady Gregory in Coole Lady
(Photograph courtesy of Sam McCready)
Design: December

Set in New Baskerville
Printed by Quinn s Printers, Belfast

For Mrs. Gill, my first teacher
For Irene Browne, who opened my eyes to what was possible
For Hilda Taggart, who taught me so much

CONTENTS

Preface

James Pethica

I

On 10th May 1932, terminally ill with cancer, Lady
Gregory signed a contract with the Putnam publishing
house granting them the right to 'arrange make selections
from and print and publish' both her autobiography,
Seventy Years, which she had worked on intermittently since
1914, and the extensive journal she had compiled since
1916.[i] It was the final literary decision of her long career.
In increasing pain, she had made her last entry in the
journal the previous day, and was thereafter no longer able
to write so much as a brief letter.[ii] Her final parting with
Yeats, who had spent most of the previous ten months at
Coole in companionable vigil with his ailing friend, came
when he left for a trip to Dublin on 12th May, though
neither knew at the time that it would be their last
meeting.[iii] She died in the early hours of 23rd May.

Lady Gregory's concern that her autobiographical
materials should be attended to promptly after her death
was the culmination of a long effort on her part to try to
influence critical and biographical responses to her life

and work. Always careful in the management of her public persona, she gave increasing creative attention in her last two decades to narratives characterising her career as a writer and cultural activist—in volumes such as *Our Irish Theatre* (1913) and *Coole* (1931), and in numerous shorter works, as well as in the materials she now assigned to Putnam. Although she routinely professed that she had written an autobiography merely to save trouble for her family and later scholars, she dreaded the prospect of invasive and inappropriate use of her papers, and deplored forms of biography that emphasised aspects of personal life she thought should remain private. Her daughter-in-law, Margaret Gregory, shrewdly observed that Lady Gregory had thus written her own 'Life' in part so as 'to forestall anyone else doing so.'[iv] Having stressed in a codicil to her will in November 1931 that the 'final decision' regarding the arrangement and publication of her papers should be 'made by my friend of so many years W.B. Yeats,'[v] and having destroyed some sensitive papers herself in the 1920s, Lady Gregory must have been confident that the agreement with Putnam would ensure discerning use of the materials, as well as guaranteeing that her own narrative accounts of her literary career would remain to the fore in the period immediately after her death.

Her expectations would end up being subverted almost completely, however. The question of how to proceed was contentious from the start, as tensions quickly surfaced between Yeats, Margaret Gregory and Putnam as to whose authority should be paramount in making 'final' decisions regarding the unpublished materials: Yeats, under the terms of a codicil that made Lady Gregory's wishes clear but which had not been signed by two witnesses and thus was not a legal document; Margaret, who had inherited Lady Gregory's copyrights; or Putnam under the terms of the 1932 contract. To make matters worse, the Putnam company's commitment to publishing the autobiography waned significantly within just a few months of Lady Gregory's death, as the deepening economic depression made commercial prospects for the volume increasingly unpromising.[vi] After lying moribund for a decade, the typescript was eventually returned to Margaret Gregory. It would not be published until 1974. As it became clear that an agreement regarding the autobiography was unlikely to be reached, Yeats began to stress in early 1933 that, in its absence, a biography of Lady Gregory must be completed as soon as possible, and by a discriminating and knowledgeable friend rather than 'some unworthy hand'.[vii] By May of that year, with no further progress having been made in agreeing on a suitable editor or biographer, he finally signalled his willingness to write a life of her himself.[viii] But this proposal, too, would prove ill-fated. Determined to safeguard the value of the autobiography, Margaret responded by insisting that Putnam should not turn over Lady Gregory's unpublished papers to Yeats for use in such a project, and that she would support only the publication of 'what Lady Gregory has herself written.'[ix]

Though probably intended largely to force Putnam's hand and spur the publication of *Seventy Years*, Margaret's decision would have two significant and unanticipated long-term consequences. Most immediate and damaging was that the opportunity for a substantial biography, to be published soon after Lady Gregory's death as Yeats had urged, was quickly lost as disagreements over use of the unpublished materials dragged on. A final, belated effort in the 1940s to redeem the situation, when Lennox Robinson was asked by his fellow-directors at the Abbey Theatre to write a biography, and was also approached by Putnam to make selections from the journal, would again flounder in conflict. Margaret considered the selections Robinson made to be a tasteless distortion of the full journal, and demeaning to Lady Gregory's memory, and they were published, over her objection, only after numerous cuts had been made at her insistence. Considering him unfit to write a biography, she also blocked Robinson's access to Lady Gregory's other unpublished papers when undertaking the work, much as she had done with Yeats. The biography he eventually completed pleased no one and duly remained unpublished.[x] It would be a full generation after Lady Gregory's death before a first substantive biography was completed by Elizabeth Coxhead in 1961—this, too, would be written largely without the use of her unpublished papers—and it is only in the last two decades or so that critical and biographical work on her has finally proliferated, and the fuller use of her massive archive begun.

The second result of Margaret's 1933 decision was more subtle, but also highly consequential. Having worked to serve Lady Gregory's interests as best he could despite the ambiguous position he faced due to the legally invalid codicil, Yeats had become increasingly frustrated by the collective failure to act on her clear wishes, and particularly by what he saw as Margaret's obstructionism. They had long been hostile to one another, and he now saw her as deliberately trying to 'prevent' him from writing a biography.[xi] His response, however, was a stately refusal to be bullied. Asserting that his 'loyalty to Lady Gregory's memory' impelled him to proceed, he declared that he would write 'an independent life of Lady Gregory for my own publishers', and would found the work on his 'own memory' rather than on the unpublished papers she had denied him access to.[xii] But in a significant shift of emphasis he also now signalled that his aim would not be strictly a 'Life' of Lady Gregory, as he had initially proposed, but instead a 'study of the whole movement' that she had participated in with him.[xiii]

The resulting volume, *Dramatis Personae,* thus unsurprisingly registers some degree of conflicted aim, as Yeats's initial desire to celebrate the career of his closest friend—and thereby 'discharge' the 'obligation of gratitude' he felt towards her[xiv]—was subsumed into his broader project of writing about a 'whole movement'. In Elizabeth Coxhead's view, far from providing Lady Gregory with a *monumentum perenne*, the volume effected an unfortunate 'elbowing-aside' in which she featured at best as an adjunct to Yeats's genius.[xv] Yeats himself was certainly uneasy about whether he had represented her adequately. In a 1934 letter to Margaret reporting progress on the work, he acknowledged that what he had written about 'Coole and Lady Gregory' was rather 'introductory', and that despite his best intentions his memories of George Moore had 'rather filled the scene'. The letter mentions a plan to expand the manuscript to double its current length—and by implication give 'Coole and Lady Gregory' their fuller due—but Yeats did not act on this aim. More revealing, still, however, is his opening to the letter, on a matter nominally unconnected with *Dramatis Personae.*

Telling Margaret that a portrait of Lady Gregory she had recently presented to the Abbey Theatre had been received, Yeats reports that the canvas had been hung right next to a considerably bigger portrait of himself. He would have this unfortunate placement rectified, he assured her, but in the meantime, 'My portrait is much larger and dwarfs Lady Gregory's portrait.'[xvi] Deliberately or not, the letter signals a realisation that his new volume might constitute a similar, unfortunate eclipse of his closest friend. Rather than there now being a free-standing biography in print to celebrate Lady Gregory's career and to present her unequivocally as the central subject of its narrative, Margaret's determined stance had resulted in there being only a subsidiary and somewhat provisional portrait of her, inseparable from and in dangerously close proximity to the 'larger' focal and compelling self-narrative of Yeats himself.

II

The difficulty of how to position a biographical canvas of Lady Gregory in relation to Yeats in particular, and of how to distinguish her achievement as an independent creative voice, from her accomplishments as friend and patron to others, more generally, has remained a core challenge in critical and biographical approaches to her career. As Sean O'Casey perceptively observed in his conflicted but affectionate recollections of her, his hardest task was in trying 'to single out the best work done by this old woman, flitting through life like a robin with the eye of a hawk; for she had as much to do with what she did not do as she had with what she did.'[xvii] Yet the very impulse to represent

Lady Gregory unequivocally as a distinct and independent identity is, as O'Casey himself clearly recognised, itself a potentially dangerous and distortive one, given the centrality of her commitment to working for, with, and through others throughout her career. Her patronage of others—whether in the form of practical work, monetary support, or creative help—was for him an essential part of her achievement, as well as paradoxically being a limiting factor which had damagingly prevented her from exploiting her own creative drives as fully as she might have: 'She loosened the tautness of her own work by taking too much time helping others, Sean thought ... indeed this serving eagerness of hers was a weakness in her nature.'[xviii] Viewed in too close proximity to the dominating presence of Yeats, or seen primarily as a facilitator and collaborator, Lady Gregory's portrait inevitably suffers—she too readily becomes just the symptomatically unnamed woman who kept the visiting creative swallows at Coole to their 'first intent': powerful and influential, but not individuated creatively.[xix] Yet the instinct to try to separate her from this milieu is to risk other kinds of distortion, since her instinct to help others, which O'Casey regretted as a 'weakness', was unambiguously as much a part of her creative identity as was her individual artistic ambition.

Yeats's cumulative mosaic portrait of her in his poems and prose works highlights the interplay between individual artistic egotism and desire to serve as being at the very core of her identity. In 'The Municipal Gallery Revisited' for instance, the 'great ebullient portrait' of her by Antonio Mancini falls short for him by failing to capture 'all that pride and that humility'—both her 'proud' aristocratic determination, constantly impelling her to strive for artistic and personal 'excellence'; and the seemingly antithetical accompanying humble, even self-effacing, impulse to help others even at the cost of her own achievement. Yeats implies in the poem that this interplay was ultimately the source of her greatest power, as well as of her distinctive character, since it allowed her in some sense to transcend the limitations of conventional gender-identification: 'I am in despair that time may bring/Approved patterns of women or of men/But not that selfsame excellence again.'[xx] He repeatedly figures her as a powerful amalgam of attributes from both genders—neither simply conventionally male in seeking to serve her own ends, nor simply conventionally female (like the generic figure in his earlier poem 'On Woman') in being willing to give 'up all her mind'[xxi] in support of male enterprise. Instead she productively combines egotistical decisiveness and collaborative generosity, raising both herself and others to greater artistic achievement. Yet for all his admiration, he was far from being able to consistently represent her in such positive terms. If 'The Municipal Gallery Revisited' manages to portray her as embodying a characteristically Yeatsian dynamic synthesis of opposing forces, many of his efforts to characterise her are evasive, provisional or fragmentary at best. The opposing forces he so carefully aligned in 'The Municipal Gallery' would elsewhere feature as merely contradictory impulses, or, at worst, be defined as preventing her from reaching true artistic intensity. During the tensions between them in 1910, when she intervened on Yeats's behalf in his application for a Civil List pension, he would roundly dismiss her 'zeal in my service' as motivated by a rigid moral code, and characterise her failure to reject 'conventional standards' as relegating her from the 'artist's world' to a world that was 'merely social.'[xxii]

Such contradictory feelings, and a sense that Lady Gregory was herself a mass of contradictions, are the hallmark of the many accounts of her given by her closest contemporaries. For Sean O'Casey, for instance, she was an impressive but unsettling amalgam of peasant and *grande dame*, of sacred and profane impulses, and of sophistication and coarseness; he first introduces her in *Inishfallen, Fare Thee Well* as being 'like an old, elegant nun of a new order, a blend of the Lord Jesus Christ and of Puck.' In a series of brilliant conceits, he then builds up a paradoxical composite portrait of her as a 'stiff gazelle,' as a combination of 'merriment and mourning' with her 'solemn black' attire offset by 'twinkling eyes', as stubborn yet conciliating, and as fundamentally courageous yet too readily swayed by personal loyalties.[xxiii] In drawing her in such conflicted terms, Yeats and O'Casey seek to portray her as unique and thus in some sense as unrepresentable, signalling their consciousness of the inevitable gap between her living individuality, in all its contradictions, and the limitations of a literary narrative. Yeats's seemingly rhetorical question in 'The Municipal Gallery Revisited' asking 'where is the brush that could show anything/Of all that pride and that humility?' surely invites the answer that no such brush can be found and that all biographical and artistic representations are doomed to be partial (in both senses of that word). But the poem notably also refuses to articulate such an answer directly, thereby signalling an unwillingness to surrender the obligation of striving to represent its subject adequately; the painter's 'brush' may fail, but the poet, using language, will continue the heroic effort to succeed.[xxiv]

All biographical (and autobiographical) enterprise inevitably faces this generic difficulty of trying to limit or disguise the size of the gap between the lived experience of the subject and the narrated life constructed from the surviving traces—fragmentary, yet still daunting—of that lived experience. As Hayden White has stressed: 'It is because real events do not offer themselves as stories that their narrativization is so difficult.'[xxv] With literary biography, that generic challenge is particularly acute, since the very creative processes which presumably make the subject of the narrative worthy of our study, are themselves the most evasive, uncertain and complex aspects of the subject's own experience. Yeats himself memorably stressed that the ordinary life of the artist and the realm they inhabit in the moment of creative making are and must be separated by a 'phantasmagoria', and that the difference between the 'bundle of accident and incoherence' who 'sits down to breakfast', and that same person now 'reborn' as the writer at work, is absolute.[xxvi] For T.S. Eliot, likewise, 'the more perfect the artist, the more completely separate in him will be the man who suffers and the mind which creates.'[xxvii] Without some form of narrativisation, we are left only with 'accident and incoherence'; but the very patterns the biographer is obliged to assert in charting dominant developments and influences in the subject's life inevitably fall short of explaining or even manifesting what Yeats described as the 'phantasmagoria' involved in the shift between ordinary experience and 'reborn' artistic making.

III

Coole Lady, written by Sam McCready and realised in performance with extraordinary power by Joan McCready, offers a superb and provocative new response to the challenge of presenting a satisfactory 'portrait' of Lady Gregory. By choosing drama rather than conventional biography as their medium, they brilliantly sidestep many of the generic limitations of scholarly narratives. A conventional biographer is obliged to make limiting choices about what aspects of the subject's life they consider most crucial, and then, directly or indirectly, to show that the account they present responds both rigorously and persuasively to the surviving evidence. But regardless of whether the biographer offers a simplified 'core' narrative' (giving immediacy and clarity, but at the risk of oversimplification) or a more complex narrative (allowing greater fidelity to the 'incoherence' and complexity of the lived experience, but at the cost of proliferating footnotes and qualifications), the biographer's interventions, and the project of narrative construction, are bound to remain obtrusively visible at every turn. In drama, by contrast, we are offered the illusion of immediate, unmediated participation in the moment of lived experience itself. That illusion is brilliantly intensified in *Coole Lady* by the strategy of having Lady Gregory narrate her life in what not only purport to be, but what actually are, in the main, her 'own' words— the text of the play is drawn almost entirely from sources in her autobiography, published and unpublished letters, her journal, diaries and other personal writings. At one stroke this strategy removes, or at least renders invisible, the presence of scholarly intervention, selectiveness and distortion: what we witness appears to be her own testimony, uncompromised by external interpretive voices. So too, as dramatic action, the play reduces, and even seems to eliminate, the usually unbridgeable gap between ordinary lived experience and the 'reborn' but elusive realm of creative making. Here, Lady Gregory's words in the play appear to function simultaneously as both ordinary experience—we see an old woman meditating, with varying levels of energy and quickly shifting emotions, on her long life—and an actual moment of artistry, in which we are allowed to see her in the process of creating an autobiographical self-portrait.

There are, of course, potential dangers as well as massive advantages in this strategy. To draw so directly on Lady Gregory's own narratives of self is to risk, most obviously, merely replicating the core components of the carefully groomed account she herself approved of, thereby failing to acknowledge and read against the artifice, self-interest and even self-deceptions lurking in those writings. The subtlety and dramatic force of *Coole Lady* stems in large part from Sam McCready's careful attention to and mediation of this potential danger. On the one hand, the text is always careful not to compromise the all-important illusion of transparency—the illusion that this is Lady Gregory herself speaking—as this is crucial to the impression of spontaneity it seeks overall. But at the same time, the play offers its audience numerous elliptical reminders that what we are watching is, indeed, merely a performance of identity on Lady Gregory's own part—a management of her own story— and thereby inevitably 'partial'. The opening of the play is particularly skilful in this respect. In almost her first few words, Lady Gregory voices regret that she is now too old for further creative or practical work, and she momentarily hesitates—'If I were certain all work was over I think I should be happy to sit still. But I'm not certain.' At face value, this faithfully reproduces her frequently-voiced unwillingness in her final months to relinquish all thought of fresh creative inspiration; but it also deftly raises the question of the artifice and creative status of what follows. This is effective drama, since it gives us the impression of momentary access to a mind in the process of trying to decide; but it also deliberately leaves the audience time to consider whether this self-presentation is indeed a spontaneous meditation as it purports to be, or is itself a creative (and hence strategic) act of self-presentation.

Other early portions of the text similarly invite us to recognise that what we are seeing is not only a 'story' but also a story that might be told in other ways or with other inflections. When the onstage Lady Gregory remembers that she was 'the runt of the family' or when she ventriloquises her older brothers' brusque demands on her, we are made directly conscious that her remembered irritation is being revealed only briefly, and not fully: the woman we listen to is conspicuously withholding the kind of larger, active, negative judgements on her family that she could clearly make if she wanted to. At first the viewer or reader may be tempted to interpret such moments simply as her generous-minded and forgiving effort to transcend her own remembered annoyances; but it becomes less possible to respond solely in these terms as the play proceeds. Revealingly, the moments in the play which most vigorously challenge the audience in this way typically come at the points where McCready intervenes most directly in modifying or supplementing the language he has drawn from Lady Gregory's own accounts. Her writings don't, for instance, offer us a moment in which she actually describes herself as 'the runt of the family' or where she puts words into her brothers' mouths detailing their demands on her time; her surviving accounts of responding to Sir William Gregory's proposal offer nothing as emphatic as the enthusiastic (and wonderfully euphonious) 'I will, Sir William, I will'; nor is there a direct archival source for her summative memories about her affair with Wilfrid Scawen Blunt—'So dangerous! So irresponsible!' These small but highly consequential interventions in no way distort the autobiographical record Lady Gregory's own writings offer us—they attend admirably to the spirit and content of those writings, in fact, and merely sharpen and intensify implications that those writings are sometimes hesitant to offer quite so directly; but they do subtly invite us to read against, or desire to read more deeply into, the narrative that the on-stage Lady Gregory offers, and thereby elliptically invite us to be on our guard as to the transparency of the larger story she tells us.

While avoiding the obtrusive interventions of the scholarly voice, the play thus carefully reminds us, in numerous ways, that the dramatic portrait we observe necessarily remains a construction and an artifice-shaped by Lady Gregory herself, most visibly (since 'her' words predominate), but by McCready too. At the moments of greatest dramatic power in *Coole Lady*, our sense that what we are seeing is directly unmediated life, and that it is also artifice, are superbly simultaneous. Lady Gregory's final speech offers perhaps the most eerie and affecting instance in the play. In her penultimate words, she casts her mind back to the 1902 drama *Cathleen ni Houlihan*, the most successful of her collaborations with Yeats, and remembers lines spoken by Cathleen, a figure for Ireland, when she first enters the peasant cottage of the Gillane family in the guise of an old woman. Lady Gregory's few words here operate, most simply, as an aging woman's affectionate memory of a moment of great creative triumph, both for herself and Yeats, and they also suggest that she is remembering having long ago played the role of Cathleen herself—as we are reminded earlier in *Coole Lady*—when an actress billed to play the part became unavailable at the last moment. But the lines also briefly transport the aged Lady Gregory, tired at the end of her life story, into the identity of Cathleen—the 'poor old woman' seemingly broken and powerless, who is transformed and renewed when she finds a hearer to give her allegiance, and who calls her audience to choose the immortality of being remembered for their service to Ireland over the more transient satisfactions of the ordinary world. Affectionate memory, Lady Gregory's self-identification with Cathleen herself, and the quiet implication that her service, too, has indeed deserved to be 'remembered for ever' compete ambiguously here as possible meanings. But McCready brilliantly complicates these already subtle implications by altering the quotations from the text of *Cathleen ni Houlihan* very slightly—'quiet feet' becomes 'tired feet' for instance, and 'many a one that doesn't make me welcome' becomes 'few that would not make me welcome.'[xxviii] Is this the accidental misquotation of a woman who no longer remembers the lines accurately, or is too tired to recall them precisely; or her wry identification with the tiredness that Cathleen feels; or a parting, somewhat regretful recognition that, for her, unlike Cathleen, no transformative rejuvenation into 'a young girl' with 'the walk of a queen' awaited? All these possibilities jostle, richly suggestive, and what we witness manages to create the illusion of both a moment of lived experience, and—more magically—suggestive access into a creative mind at work.

As its title suggests, *Coole Lady* is motivated at root by admiration of Lady Gregory's achievements as a writer, a practical force in Irish cultural life, and a patron and friend who collaborated with and helped many of the ablest creative minds in the Ireland of her time. In so far as it is an act of homage, its form—a one act drama—is one which Lady Gregory herself would surely have appreciated, given that her own greatest creative work came as a dramatist. The narrative Sam McCready has crafted here covers the core terrain of her career with affection, economy and insight, and richly augments the 'portrait' of her that has previously been available. The play is highly conscious of its own artifice, and of the fact that one can never truly 'recreate' an actual life on stage; but McCready has exploited his medium to the full, and audiences fortunate enough to see this work in performance will be treated, at least briefly, to the illusion of Lady Gregory not only speaking for herself, but directly to us.

James Pethica, Williams College, is working on the authorised biography of Lady Gregory

[i] Lady Gregory, *Seventy Years*, ed. Colin Smythe (New York: Macmillan, 1974), pp.v-vii

[ii] *Lady Gregory's Journals: Volume Two*, ed. Daniel J. Murphy (New York: Oxford University Press, 1987), p.631

[iii] Yeats (hereafter WBY) to George Yeats, 10th May 1932, in *The Collected Letters of W.B. Yeats* (InteLex electronic edition, 2002), John Kelly, General Editor

[iv] Colin Smythe, 'Afterword', in *Lady Gregory's Journals: Volume Two*, p.648

[v] Ibid. p.645

[vi] *Seventy Years*, p.viii

[vii] WBY to T.J. Kiernan, 17th March 1933 (InteLex)

[viii] WBY to George Yeats, 16th June 1933 (InteLex)

[ix] Ibid

[x] Colin Smythe, 'Afterword', in *Lady Gregory's Journals: Volume Two*, p.656-60

[xi] WBY to George Yeats, 16th June 1933 (InteLex)

[xii] Ibid. WBY to Margaret Gough, 27 June 1933, and WBY to Lady Gregory's Executors, 27th June 1933 (InteLex)

[xiii] WBY to Margaret Gough, 27th June 1933 (InteLex)

[xiv] WBY to Margaret Gough, 24th October 1933 (InteLex)

[xv] Elizabeth Coxhead, *Lady Gregory: A Literary Portrait* (London: Macmillan, 1961), pp.218-19

[xvi] WBY to Margaret Gough, 24th November 1934 (InteLex)

[xvii] Sean O'Casey, *Inishfallen, Fare Thee Well* (New York: Macmillan, 1949), p.194

[xviii] Ibid. p.196

[xix] *The Variorum Edition of the Poems of W. B. Yeats*, eds. Peter Allt and Russell K. Alspach (New York: Macmillan, 1966), p.489 (hereafter VP)

[xx] VP, p.602

[xxi] VP, p.345

[xxii] W.B. Yeats, *Memoirs*, ed. Denis Donoghue (New York: Macmillan, 1972), pp.255-58

[xxiii] *Inishfallen, Fare Thee Well*, pp.163, 182-195.

[xxiv] VP, p.602

[xxv] Hayden White, *The Content of the Form: Narrative Discourse and Historical Representation* (Baltimore: Johns Hopkins, 1987), p.24

[xxvi] W.B. Yeats, *Essays and Introductions* (New York: Macmillan, 1961), p.509

[xxvii] T.S. Eliot, *Selected Essays* (London: Faber, 1951), p.18

[xxviii] *The Variorum Edition of the Plays of W. B. Yeats*, ed. Russell K. Alspach (London: Macmillan, 1966), pp. 222, 231

Acknowledgements

Writing this play has given me an enormous amount of pleasure, firstly because of the subject itself, the indomitable Lady Gregory, and secondly because it allowed me the opportunity to work with my wife, Joan, whose performance of the 'Coole Lady' was an inspiration to me and to the many who saw her when the show toured in Ireland and the United States. Not only did Joan bring the words of Lady Gregory to life but she was also centrally involved in the whole project, offering advice on the mood and tone of the writing and being very forthright about what she felt Lady Gregory would or would not reveal to the listener. This is her play as much as mine. Martin Lynch, a dear friend, was willing to take a chance with an aspiring playwright and did a mammoth job in producing the play and ensuring it had audiences in all the venues in which it played in Ireland, north and south. In this, he was supported by Anne-Marie Murray, the administrator, Green Shoot Productions. Words cannot describe how hard she worked for this play. I am grateful to Jonathan Allison, Director of the Yeats International Summer School, and to Maura McTighe and all the members of the Yeats Society in Sligo. *Coole Lady* premiered in Sligo in August 2003, and the students and faculty at the summer school gave it a rousing send-off at that first performance in the Model Arts and Niland Gallery. It was in Sligo that I met one of the foremost authorities on Lady Gregory, James Pethica, who has generously written the preface. From the moment I shared the script with him, he has been intensely supportive. He has answered my questions, advised me gently when something I had written was wrong, and given me such encouragement that I dared send him rewrites for his approval. He was unfailingly helpful, courteous, kind, and I thank him from the bottom of my heart. Other Gregory scholars, too, have given help and encouragement. Lucy McDiarmid was there from the beginning. When I tentatively e-mailed her, telling her that I was thinking of writing a play on Lady Gregory, she responded enthusiastically and provided a list of important sources. Her comments on the performance at Chestertown, New York, in September 2004, were very helpful. Maureen Murphy, too, shared her infectious enthusiasm for the project. Christopher Griffin, whose grandfather worked for Lady Gregory and is mentioned in her journals, made helpful suggestions when he heard an early draft of the play, which at that stage was a two-hander! Andy McGowan of the New York Yeats Society, and his wife, Judy, have been totally supportive. I would also like to thank all those who contributed to the writing and the presentation, most often by their friendship and willingness to help in whatever way they could, especially Sue Brander, Terry Cobb, Tony Coughlan, Desmond Cranston, Robert Crone, Edith Devlin, Deborah and Roger Doherty, James Eckert, Cathy Fagan, Steven Fischer, Declan Foley, Ellis Foy, Philip Johnston, Cathy Kafir, Richard and Janis Londraville, Mark Luce, Jay and Eve

Mateer, Maire O'Brien, Sr. Olive McConville, Paddy O'Flaherty, Gloria Patton, Chrissie Poulter, Doug Saum, Greggory Schraven, Moore and Sandra Sinnerton, Denis Smyth, and Dorothy Wiley. My thanks are due, too, to the administrators and staff of all the theatres in which the play has been performed, and to all those audiences who responded so overwhelmingly to Lady Gregory's story. I am also indebted to the Arts Council of Northern Ireland who partly funded the initial Irish tour with an Awards for All grant. I am grateful to the staff of the New York Public Library for allowing me access to the Gregory papers in the Berg Collection, and to Declan Kiely who facilitated my research there. Above all, I should like to acknowledge the generosity and support of Colin Smythe who has done so much to promote the work of Lady Gregory and to ensure its survival. He has kindly allowed me to quote material from Lady Gregory's autobiography and journals for which he holds the copyright, and I thank him.

I have dedicated the play to three of my teachers. All were special women who made a difference in the lives of many—as Lady Gregory did. Indeed, I would wish to acknowledge the many teachers, too many to name individually, who gave me so much and to whom I am increasingly grateful.

Sam McCready
March 2005

Bibliography

The first biography of Lady Gregory appeared in 1961. While working on a book about women authors, the English novelist Elizabeth Coxhead was surprised to find nothing significant had been written about Lady Gregory and she set about rectifying the omission. Her book, *Lady Gregory: A Literary Portrait*, was my introduction to the life of the 'chatelaine of Coole' and I will always have great affection for it. There have been a number of biographies since, including Mary Lou Kohfeldt's *Lady Gregory: The Woman Behind the Irish Renaissance* (1985), and the most recent, Colm Toibin's highly readable and engaging *Lady Gregory's Toothbrush* (2003). All have benefited from the Coole Editions of Lady Gregory's writings, including her journals and diaries, published by Colin Smythe.

In working on the play *Coole Lady*, I found the following books by or about Lady Gregory of value. I would also wish to acknowledge *Gort Inse Guaire: A Journey Through Time*, edited by Marguerite Grey and Marie McNamara for the Gort Heritage Trust, 2000.

WORKS BY LADY GREGORY—THE COOLE EDITION

Our Irish Theatre, foreword by Roger McHugh, 1972

Seventy Years, 1852-1922, edited with a foreword by Colin Smythe, 1974

The Journals, Vol. 1, edited by Daniel J. Murphy, 1978

The Journals, Vol. II, edited by Daniel J. Murphy, 1987

WORKS BY LADY GREGORY—OTHER EDITIONS

Coole, completed from the manuscript and edited by Colin Smythe. Dublin: Dolmen, 1971

Lady Gregory's Diaries 1892-1902, edited James Pethica. Gerrards Cross: Colin Smythe, 1996

Selected Writings, edited by Lucy McDiarmid and Maureen Waters. London: Penguin, 1995

WORKS ABOUT LADY GREGORY

Frazier, Adrian. *Behind the Scenes: Yeats, Horniman, and the Struggle for the Abbey Theatre*. Berkeley: University of California Press, 1990

Gregory, Anne. *Me and Nu: Childhood at Coole*. Gerrards Cross: Colin Smythe, 1970

Mikhail, E.H. ed. *Lady Gregory: Interviews & Recollections*. Totowa, N.J.: Rowman & Littlefield, 1977

Saddlemyer, Ann & Smythe, Colin, eds. *Lady Gregory, Fifty Years After*. Gerrards Cross: Colin Smythe, 1987

Smythe, Colin. *A Guide to Coole Park, Home of Lady Gregory*. Gerrards Cross: Colin Smythe, 1973

Chronology

1852 *Birth of Augusta Gregory (née Persse) at Roxborough, Co. Galway*

1878 *Death of father, Dudley Persse*

1880 *Marries Sir William Gregory of Coole Park*

1881 *Birth of son, William Robert, in London*

1882 *Begins love affair with Wilfrid Scawen Blunt*

1892 *Death of Sir William. Sells London residence and returns to Coole*

1897 *W.B. Yeats spends the first of twenty summers at Coole*

1899 *First performance of Irish Literary Theatre*

1902 *Publication of* Cuchulain of Muirthemne

1903 *Her first play,* Twenty Five, *produced by Irish National Theatre Society*

1904 *Opening of the Abbey Theatre*

1907 *Robert marries Margaret Graham Parry*

1909 *Birth of Richard Graham Gregory, her first grandchild*

1911 *Birth of second grandchild, Augusta Anne Gregory. Travels with the Abbey Theatre production of* The Playboy of the Western World *to America*

1912 *Has a brief love affair with John Quinn in New York*

1913 *Birth of Catherine Frances Gregory, her third grandchild*

1915 *Death of her nephew, Sir Hugh Lane, on* S.S. Lusitania

1917 *Yeats buys Thoor Ballylee, adjacent to Coole Park, and marries Georgie Hyde Lees*

1918 *Death of Robert, shot down in error while on a flying mission over Italy. Buried in Padua*

1919 *Plays title role in* Cathleen ni Houlihan *at the Abbey Theatre*

1923 *First operation for breast cancer*

1924 *Family home at Roxborough burned to the ground*

1926 *Second operation for breast cancer under local anaesthetic*

1927 *Coole Park sold to the Forestry Commission. Leases Coole House*

1928 *Margaret Gregory marries Captain Guy Gough of Lough Cutra*

1932 *Dies at Coole Park. Buried in the New Cemetery, Galway*

COOLE LADY

Coole Lady was first performed at the Yeats International Summer School, Sligo, 3rd August 2003. It was subsequently produced on tour in Ireland, June and October 2004, by Green Shoot Productions, Belfast. The play was directed and designed by Sam McCready. The cast and crew were as follows:

Lady Gregory	Joan McCready
Producer	Martin Lynch
Administrator	Anne-Marie Murray
Production Manager	Mags Mulvey/Elaine Barnes

The New York premiere was produced by Handcart Ensemble (J. Scott Reynolds, Artistic Director; Kevin Ashworth, Managing Director), at Theatre 315, 315 W. 47th Street, 20th-30th April 2005. Joan McCready again played the role of Lady Gregory.

The play is a monologue in one act and takes place in the drawing room of Lady Gregory's home at Coole Park, County Galway. The time is the early 1931.

The drawing room of Lady Gregory's home at Coole Park. There is a comfortable Victorian armchair, a pile of books on a small table beside the chair, and a desk on which are family pictures and a box of letters. Lady Gregory enters, supporting herself with a walking stick. She looks nostalgically at the pictures and then speaks.

LADY GREGORY: I suppose in my seventy-ninth year I should be content to sit still and meditate on the life that's past and the unseen life to come. My bodily strength is lessening, the morning uprising less buoyant, and the evening reading has its danger signals up against small type. But I don't grumble or complain. I have had a full life, a happy life, apart from its two great griefs. I have served my country, my darlings and my friends. If I were certain all work was over, I think I should be happy just to sit still. But I'm not certain.

Augusta Gregory—co-founder of the Abbey Theatre, poet, playwright, folklorist, mother, grandmother, Nationalist—I was with the Nationalists all through—more than they knew or my nearest realised. Up the Rebels! I had no education worth talking about and as a child I was shy and withdrawn. At my first dinner party at the Goughs, I was too shy to ask for the salt and had a thoroughly unappetising meal.

I was born at Roxborough, a big country house in County Galway, in March 1852, daughter of Dudley Persse. My father owned thousands of acres but he was confined to a wheelchair because of gout and his fondness for the drink.

By reputation, he was a bigot and a proselytizer. He tried to convert every Catholic—man, woman and child in the district. In this, he was ably supported by my mother, a staunch evangelical Protestant who believed that all sin was terrible but that if you were saved, sin didn't really matter.

I was the fifth daughter of my mother, and although she had four sons, besides a stepson, she liked boys better than girls, and so when I was born she was sorry I wasn't a boy. Rejected as soon as I took my first breath of this world's air, I was mislaid among the bed quilts, and only the thoughtfulness of an old nurse saved me from suffocation. I was named Isabella Augusta, after a never-to-be-seen godmother, a Miss Brown of Bath. I grew up short and plain, the runt of the family, more at ease with my four rambunctious younger brothers than with my ladylike and attractive sisters, who, like me, had little formal education. But my mother insisted that we learn good manners and a smattering of French. The Bible was read every day, there was church twice on Sunday and daily prayers.

A life of service, whether to family or a wealthy husband, was expected of the Persse sisters. But for me, the homely Augusta, it seemed certain to be a life of service to my hunting and shooting brothers. 'Augusta! Have you seen my riding crop?' 'A brace of pheasants, Augusta. See that they're plucked and hung so that we can have them for dinner next week!'

After dinner each evening, we would retire to the drawing room for family prayers. All of the family and many of the household gathered there, but not the old nurse or other Catholic servants—God forbid! After the prayers were over, a silver urn was brought, and Mama, or the Mistress as we called her, made tea. There was no conversation in which all might join; there was silence except when my sister played on the piano or Mama read aloud from the London *Times*. But when there were dinner parties, there was a greater joy to be found, for then the great centre table would be covered with a cloth of velvet pile and a few carefully kept books in handsome bindings would be brought out and laid upon it, chief among them a volume of English ballads, a never failing treasury of delight. And of these the most stirring was 'Chevy Chase', memorable not only for the unforgettable dauntlessness of its hero but also because my family, the Persses, claimed descent from the Persses of the ballad. That ballad book, and some poems of Wordsworth on shiny paper, and a volume of Shakespeare in small print that I was forbidden to read by my mother until I was older; these treasures were taken away by my sister when she married, but they were not entirely out of reach, for they adorned the drawing room table of her estate at Castle Taylor, about five or six miles to the north west of Roxborough. And there I could read Shakespeare to my heart's content: 'Come to my woman's breasts and take my milk for gall, you murdering ministers ... '

When I was eighteen, I bought a Shakespeare for myself, the Globe edition. I learned the sonnets at my dressing table, repeating them aloud on the mountainside. And once, a wild undergraduate of Trinity College, brought on a visit by my wilder brother, shared my literary enthusiasms. But my elders soon interrupted that companionship, those delightful conversations. There was an abrupt banishment, a sudden silence. My heart hadn't been wounded nor had my hand trembled at the parting, but I now and again blush at the recollection.

From my old nurse, Mary Sheridan, who remembered the French landing at Killala in 1798, I heard stories of the brave Irish rebels, and had my first lessons in Irish, at which I later became quite proficient. Part of the romance of my early days was the whispered rumours of the servants and the overheard talk of my elders about the threatened rising of the Fenians. So it came about that I would bring out the sixpences, earned if memory held good by repeating on Sunday evenings Bible verses learned during the week; and standing on tiptoe at the counter of the little bookshop in Loughrea, I would purchase one by one the paper-covered editions of the national ballads: *The Harp of Tara* and *The Irish Song Book*. Then the shopkeeper would whisper, 'I always look to Miss Augusta to buy all my Fenian books!'

It was perhaps that remark that led to a birthday present, *The Spirit of the Nation*, a shilling copy, bound in green cloth, from my older sister. She couldn't refrain from writing in it—'Patriotism is the last refuge of the scoundrel!'

Oh! The French are on the sea,
Says the Shan Van Vocht
The French are on the sea,
Says the Shan Van Vocht
Oh! The French are in the Bay,

They'll be here without delay,
And the Orange will decay,
Says the Shan Van Vocht.

I was drawn to rebel Ireland by the wide beauty of my
home, from whose hillsides I could see the mountains of
the Burren and Iar Connacht, and at sunset, the silver
western sea ...

And will Ireland then be free?
Says the Shan Van Vocht
Will Ireland then be free?
Says the Shan Van Vocht
Yes! Ireland will be free,
From the centre to the sea,
Then hurrah for Liberty!
Says the Shan Van Vocht.

When I was twenty-six, my father died unexpectedly. I was
nursing a younger brother who had pleurisy. One lunch-
time, going to the dining room for something I needed, I
heard one of those at the table say that during the night
the cry of the banshee had been heard; and although
looking on such tales as idle, anxiety about my brother
made me feel a sudden dread. In the evening, he was still
quite ill, and towards midnight when he had fallen asleep,
I heard voices, and going to the staircase saw a group of
the servants and asked them not to make any noise. One
among them came up the stairs to me and said, 'Ma'am,
the Master is dead.'

To those of us still living under that roof, it seemed as if all
had been shattered around us. Roxborough had been
such a hive of life—with its stables full of horses, its

kennels full of sporting dogs, the sawmill with its carpenters and engineers and turners; and the garden, so well tilled, so full at that September time of grapes and melons and peaches and apples, inexhaustible fruit. Now the life seemed to have gone out of it. My half-brother Dudley was now lord of all and impatient to take possession. What would we do? Where would we go? Were we who had been rich now poor? My mother took a house in Dublin, and my life of service to my hunting and shooting brothers began. 'A brace of pheasants, Augusta. See that they're plucked and hung for dinner next week.'

And it was at that point that fate or luck or the good God intervened. An older brother was sickly with tuberculosis and I accompanied him to Cannes for the good of his health. There I renewed my acquaintance with an elderly neighbour of ours—Sir William Gregory, owner of Coole Park, an estate some seven miles from Roxborough—recently widowed, and retired from his post as Governor of Ceylon. When we returned to Galway, he sought opportunities for us to meet, and about a year later, I received a letter from him.

She takes a letter from the box on the desk and reads

'Miss Persse, may I say something that may appear presumptuous. If it offends, please tell me and it won't be spoken again. You have been admirably brought up; you're clever and well informed. You may think it foolish at my time of life to be asking for a lady's hand in marriage, especially when the lady is young enough to be my daughter. But I'll ask the question anyway. Will you be my wife? You needn't give me your answer right away.'

Coole was a large, three-storied, eighteenth-century house set in acres of parkland. It was crowded with books, paintings and mementoes of generations of Gregorys who had been soldiers and statesmen. To move from Roxborough to Coole would be to move from a world of foxhunts and horse races to one of culture, learning and society. I would be mistress of my own house. 'I will, Sir William, I will!' And I married Sir William Gregory in the Protestant church of St. Matthias in Dublin.

> Till death us part
> So speaks the heart
> When each to each repeats the words of doom
> Through blessings and through curse
> For better or for worse
> We will be one till that dread hour come.

I was 27 and he was 63. I wore a grey hat and grey travelling dress but I have always felt sorry I didn't, no matter how quiet the wedding, wear white, with wreath and veil. I feel it was a break of tradition, something missing from my life.

We honeymooned in France, Greece and Italy, the first of many travels overseas. I bought dresses in London and Paris, then we travelled to Naples where we embarked for Constantinople, then on to the Black Sea, and Scutari with its Crimean War cemetery decorated with Judas trees.

In a little over a year, our only child was born. I was hosting a luncheon for friends in our London residence. After the meal, I whispered to Lady Layard that my confinement had already begun. She promptly ordered everyone to leave, and at 9 o'clock that evening, we were blessed with a son, William Robert. I was overjoyed, but Sir William was not so happy. My confinement had caused him to cancel travel plans and he had overheard sniggers at the club.

Months later, we left Robert with my sister and set sail for Egypt. And it was there I first felt the real excitement of politics, for we tumbled into a revolution, a revolution led by Arabi Bey against the British Empire. Sir William and I were sympathetic to the anti-imperialist cause. I also met a fellow sympathiser, Wilfrid Scawen Blunt, the English poet who dressed as a Bedouin in flowing robes and seduced almost every woman he encountered. I was no exception. He was tall, lithe and handsome—radiant. I found him irresistible. By the end of a year, we had tumbled into a relationship. I was helping him with his political campaign and writing letters to the *Times* so we'd plenty of opportunity to be together. Sir William didn't suspect a thing, or if he did, he kept silent. With that one exception, I was always a good wife to my elderly husband. But a woman has passions and there are occasions when it is impossible not to give in. Our affair lasted for nearly a year until we agreed it must end. So dangerous! So irresponsible!

I chronicled my feelings for him in a series of twelve sonnets—a kind of farewell to our passion, as it were. I put them in his hand the morning we parted after our last night together in the room above the bow window of his house at Crabbet.

Later, he published them under his own name—having tidied them up, improved them, you might say.

She chooses one of the sonnets from a book on the small table beside her armchair and reads

If the past year were offered me again
And choice of good and ill before me set
Would I accept the pleasure with the pain
Or dare to wish that we had never met?
Ah! Could I bear those happy hours to miss
When love began, unthought of and unspoke—
That summer day when by a sudden kiss
We knew each other's secret and awoke?

It was a moment's glimpse of Paradise. Later I was filled with regret but I gained a little charity for weakness in others; how dare I fling the first stone. Sir William died in March 1892. We had been married twelve years, almost to the day. There was a snowstorm on the morning of his funeral. All of the tenants turned out, and the workmen carried his lead-lined coffin from Coole to the mausoleum at Kiltartan. The Protestant minister conducted the service but the Catholic bishop and all of the local clergy were there to see him off. As one of the workers said, 'He was a good man. He'll always have a green sod to stand on in the next world.'

When my husband was alive, he and I spent most of the year socialising in London, returning only for the summers to Coole. When he died, I sold our London home and returned to my family at Roxborough. My brother William, a heavy drinker, who had inherited the estate on the death of my half-brother Dudley, ordered me out. 'I know you! You're a schemer and conniver. Take yourself and your child out of my house!' On the last night of the saddest year of my life, in bitter cold, Robert and I were forced to leave my family home and take refuge in the Croft in Galway. There was a terrible difference in my life.

I decided to live permanently at Coole. When I returned, the old house and park looked dreary—but I knew I must try to stay on and do my best by it. My husband left the estate to our son Robert (he was eleven at the time) with the understanding that I might remain there throughout my lifetime. One of my first acts when I returned was to pay off my husband's debts (he had been profligate in his youth) so that my son's inheritance would be debt free. I devoted time to editing my husband's autobiography and the letters of his grandfather, and I began restoring the splendid woodlands, the seven woods, whose names if written down were matter for a sonnet by Willie Yeats— Shan-walla, Kyle-dortha, Kyle-na-no, Pairc-na-lee, Pairc-na-carraig, Pairc-na-tarav, Inchy Wood—'Seven odours, seven murmurs, seven woods.'

I first met William Butler Yeats in London a few years after the death of Sir William but our friendship dates from his first visit to Coole two years later. He was on a walking tour of the west of Ireland with his friend Arthur Symons. They were staying with Edward Martyn at his castle at Tillyra, and I invited them to Coole for lunch.

I was especially struck by young Yeats. With his tall gait and dreamy eyes, he looked every inch the poet. I'd read his *Celtic Twilight* and envied Sligo that it had found its voice. 'Why don't we collect folklore together here in Galway?' I said. 'You could remain here for a time at Coole while your friend returns to London.'

He came back the following summer, and I brought him from cottage to cottage gathering tales of fairies and the like. Then I typed them on one of those newfangled typewriting machines that Lady Layard had given me—a Remington. Very good training if I ever wanted to become a private secretary. We heard tales of changelings and of Biddy Early, a legend in these parts for spells and healing. In his black outfit, with him so tall, the locals thought Yeats was a Protestant missionary until Father Fahy told them not to be so superstitious!

He spent many summers at my house. Around him I created a sense of order. He slept in the master bedroom and I piled layers of carpets on the landing so that he wouldn't be disturbed by the galumphing of the maids on the staircase. 'Insist that I work every day at eleven,' he said, 'I doubt I will do much with my life but for your firmness and care.'

It was during the summer of '97 that we first discussed the possibility of a theatre where the plays of Mr. Yeats and Edward Martyn might be performed. Yeats spoke about his dream of having a theatre in London, and Martyn thought of Germany! 'Why not Dublin?' I said. 'The proper place for Irish plays is Dublin.' 'There are no actors for serious plays in Dublin,' said Yeats. 'We'll bring them from London,' I said. 'There's no money for theatre in Dublin,' insisted Yeats. 'I'll write to my friends!' And with that conversation on a wet afternoon in County Galway, the Irish Literary Theatre began. Other writers quickly joined our endeavour; chief among them at the time was George Moore, a Mayoman, fresh from success as a novelist in Paris.

When Moore told me that Yeats and he were collaborating on a heroic drama to be written on the subject of Diarmuid and Grania, I was not enthusiastic. I told him,

'Yeats's volume *The Wind Among the Reeds* was finished here last year; it would never have been finished if I hadn't invited him to Coole. There's the table at which he writes—the clean pens, the fresh ink, the spotless blotter— these are my special care every morning. And although we live in an ungrateful world, I think that some day, somebody will throw a kind word after me for *The Wind Among the Reeds.* No, I think it's hardly wise for him to undertake any collaboration with you at the moment. It's best for him to work alone.' And with that, I excused myself to go see to his lunch! That squashed that idea—for a time.

I can't say I ever took to George Moore, but Yeats was a most charming companion, never out of humour, gentle, interested in all that was going on, doing his work in the library in the midst of all the comings and goings. Then, if I was typing here in the drawing room, he would suddenly burst in with some great new idea. With me, he discovered one who understood the capacity of his mind, and could evoke it, and who never wearied of it.

> They came like swallows, and like swallows went,
> And yet a woman's powerful character
> Could keep a swallow to its first intent ...

His words ... his words! Another swallow who visited Coole at this time was Douglas Hyde. He was second only to Yeats in my affections. I met him the first time at Tillyra, pushing a broken bicycle. He was a big, affable man, with a walrus moustache, and he was welcome in any house in the west, patron or pauper. He was full of enthusiasm for the Irish language. His vision, as he founded the Gaelic League, was for a non-political movement that would restore our national pride, and he succeeded.

John Millington Synge came to Coole but he didn't seem to settle here. Too many trees, I suppose—and too much Yeats! George Bernard Shaw was affectionate and amusing. Jack Yeats came on occasions but he was most at home with the workers around the estate, joining them in the pub and standing them a drink, so different from his brother. And gentle John Masefield, the seafarer. He had grown up beside woods in England and felt at home here. I should have been content to have had him and Jack Yeats here for six months of the year, but a few weeks of their wives made me hide in the woods.

Hyde, Shaw, Synge, Russell, Yeats, Masefield, all carved their names on the copper beech that stands at the edge of the great lawn. I was selective about who signed it and offended many who thought it was the visitors' book! I was just in time to restrain the penknives of some young Americans but I later thought I was too rash; that some day in that wonder-country there might be a President in the White House whose name I had disallowed. And all the while I was entertaining these famous writers, I was running a household and a farm, and trying to spend a few hours each morning on my own writing.

I collaborated with Yeats on some of his early plays—although my name didn't make it on to the title page. Yeats never took me seriously as a writer until I showed him my *Cuchulain of Muirthemne*. 'The best book to have come out of Ireland in my time,' he said. 'In fact, the best book ever to have come out of Ireland.' Praise indeed!

But most of all, I was preoccupied with the setting up of the Irish Literary Theatre. I wanted to do something practical to help Yeats. Our plans were unexpectedly blocked by the impossibility of getting a licensed theatre in Dublin because we couldn't afford it—and anyone putting on a play in an unlicensed concert hall would be fined £300. Only an act of parliament could remedy that situation, and I'm proud to say we got that act passed! We asked friends to contribute to a guarantee fund. With varying degrees of enthusiasm for an Irish dramatic movement, we received promises of a pound here and a pound there. Indeed, the only actual refusals were from three members of the House of Lords! In the event, we didn't need the guarantee. Edward Martyn covered all our losses, and the first performance of the Irish Literary Theatre, using English actors who rehearsed in London, took place in the Antient Concert Rooms in Dublin. The public came, and most of the reviews were enthusiastic. We continued our experiment for three years, and hesitated what to do next. It was hard work but the time had come to play more often and to train actors of our own. With the help of the Fay brothers, Frank and William, who already had a small amateur company, the actors were trained and a school of Irish acting evolved.

And in 1904, a patent for a new theatre, the Abbey Theatre, was granted to Dame Augusta Gregory:

She picks up a framed copy of the patent from the desk and reads

'You are hereby enjoined and commanded to gather, entertain, govern, and keep a company of players, and not to put on stage any exhibition of wild beasts or dangerous performances or to allow women or children to be hung from the flies or fixed in positions from which they cannot release themselves.'

I was happy to comply, and comply I did; no woman was ever hung from the flies although there were a few I would have been happy to see strung from the rafters—like the Englishwoman we have to thank for the gift of the Abbey Theatre, Miss Annie Horniman, whose family made its fortune in tea. She spent about £13,000 on converting the old Mechanics' Institute in Dublin, money we could never have raised in Ireland. She had seen our Irish players when they appeared in London and was so impressed that she promised us a theatre. Now, she may well have been impressed with the players but the real reason for her generosity was Yeats. She was infatuated with him and she thought the nearest way to his heart was to give him a theatre. He never had any notion of her and it was a struggle to keep him out of her clutches, but we needed the money, even though she kept it in a tub of electrified water! The Saxon shilling! I wrote to Yeats over and over, 'She's a mad woman, a raving lunatic, insane.' She was condescending and a bully, and I was happy when she finally left us; the Fairy Godmother got back into her red, white and blue coach.

As I think back on it, I marvel at how much of my time and energy I spent and, as it seems to me, squandered, on the endless affairs of the Abbey: the effort to maintain discipline, the staging of the plays, the reading of the plays, the choice of plays, the suspicion of politicians and the authorities, anxieties about money. At the theatre I often had to act as peacemaker; sometimes there seemed to be nothing but rows. To Yeats I wrote about the trouble that was to cause me more distress than any in those early years—the quarrel with the Fays about who should run the theatre—the two of them or the two of us. Well, it had to be us, and so we lost the Fays. 'They came like swallows, and like swallows went.'

Once, when circumstances delayed the arrival at the theatre of the actress who was to play Cathleen Ni Houlihan, I horrified Yeats and the assembled company by calmly announcing that I would play the part myself. 'All that's needed is a hag and a voice!' I said.

When I went on the stage it was a shock to find the auditorium in black darkness. I thought for a moment the curtain was down and I hesitated. But, sure, I got through all right. And Yeats came up to the gallery afterwards and said coldly, 'It was very good, but if I had rehearsed you it would have been much better.'

Despite the demands of running a theatre, I spent as much of my time as possible at Coole where there was work to be done—rooms to be cleaned, workers to be paid, trees to be planted, neighbours to be fed. As one of the locals said, 'She has a power of land.' I'd five acres on the front lawn alone! I used to put up over twenty acres of hay down by the river. There was another forty acres beyond the river at Lisheencranagh, as well as the woods. Almost 2000 acres. All that took some looking after.

And all over the country at that time, there were tensions between the landlords and tenants; Roxborough had to be protected by armed guards. I'm proud to say there was never any trouble at Coole but I had to work at it. Famous people came to visit me but the not-so-famous came as well—people like Mike Power, the basket maker from Crowe Lane in Gort, Padraig Niland, the storyteller, and old Curley the piper. Everyone was welcome at Coole, the pauper as well as the gentleman. No one was ever turned away from this house empty-handed.

When my son Robert married, I had a slight nervousness about the advent of his wife, Margaret, a Welsh girl, to Coole. Happy as I was about her, it was bound to make a difference. I had been so free and unquestioned. But she was charming and beautiful and I was quite satisfied with his choice although I can't pretend there weren't tensions, especially because of Yeats. She resented him and the attention he got here. There is a large bed of sedum in the flower garden, and all summer long it'd be alive with butterflies, and I once heard Margaret remark that the sedum flowered all year round and while it was in flower, Yeats would be at Coole. She and Robert had three children and when they were abroad, I took care of the little chicks. Richard, the eldest, went off to boarding school in England but Catherine and Anne knew no other life but that of the estate. To them I was no grand lady or friend of the famous. I was Grandma!

They got into all kinds of mischief that they thought Grandma knew nothing about, like climbing trees, chasing rabbits, and fighting off the renegade Indians that threatened the Alamo. 'Little savages,' their Mama called them. Sometimes I took them with me when I went up to the Abbey and everyone made a great fuss of them. There wasn't a nook or cranny in the whole theatre they didn't find their way in to, and often when it was time to leave for

the train, they were nowhere to be found. I remember
coming home from a trip to America with a present for the
little chicks—a big basket of grapes and bananas and
grapefruit and oranges—and they carried the exotic fruit
to picnics in the woods in the elastic legs of their knickers.
I taught them to read and write—and also Arithmetic and
French. I wasn't very good at Arithmetic, so when they
finally went to school, they were put in the lowest form for
Maths; but they used to get very good marks in English
and Scripture. Their French was quite good too—despite
their Galway accent.

Our haven of family life was disturbed by the death of my
nephew, Hugh Lane, the art dealer. He was returning from
a business trip to America, when his ship, the *Lusitania*,
was torpedoed by the Germans. He had left a collection of
Impressionist paintings to the National Gallery in London
but added an unwitnessed codicil to his will leaving them
to Ireland. I fought tirelessly to have that codicil
recognised but in vain; the paintings were hung in
London.

She searches for a letter from the box on the desk and reads

'Dear Lady Gregory,
At the request of Lord Edward Carson, I have enclosed
the report of the committee appointed by the House of
Lords to determine whether the codicil appended to
your nephew Sir Hugh Lane's will has legal force. While
sympathetic to the moral argument that the pictures
should be returned to Ireland, the committee has
unequivocally decided that legally the pictures must
remain in London. I am told on good authority that had

your nephew been spared to witness the new Tate Gallery at Millbank, where the pictures will be hung, no doubt can be entertained that he would have destroyed the codicil. And there I'm afraid the matter must rest. We fought hard but we must have the graciousness to admit defeat.'

Never! I have never ceased agitating for their return.

Three years after the death of Hugh Lane, occurred the great tragedy of my life, the death of my beloved Robert, returning from a flying mission over Italy a few weeks before the end of the war. I had been in Dublin at a meeting about the Lane pictures. I was vexed because in my absence from Coole, timber had been given away, and there were men cutting the young ash that I thought Robert would enjoy seeing on his next leave. Next morning I was at my writing table here in the drawing room when Marian the maid came in, very slowly. She had a telegram in her hand and gave it to me. It was addressed to Mrs. Gregory, and I thought, 'This is telling of Robert's death. It's to his wife they've sent it.' The first words I saw were, 'Killed in action' and then, at the top, 'Deeply regret'. I said, 'How can I tell her?' for Margaret was in Galway with the children, staying with my sister. I went upstairs and put up my things for the journey, even changing my dress. Then I came down and got into the carriage and drove to the station at Gort. In the train I felt it was cruel to be going so quickly to break Margaret's heart, I wanted the train to go more slowly. At Galway I took a carriage and drove to the house. It was agony knowing the journey was at an end. A maid opened the door. I asked if Mrs. Gregory was in, and she said, 'Yes

ma'am, in the study with the mistress.' I went to the
drawing room and told the maid to send her to me. I stood
there, and Margaret came in.

'Is he dead?'

I nodded and then we both sat down on the floor and cried.

She picks up a photograph of Robert from the desk

His had been such a promising life: a talented painter, a
fine horseman, a fearless airman. He loved Ireland and I
felt certain he would have done much with his life.

The next months were lonely months. Returning to Coole
after being in Dublin was always sad and depressing; the
silence, and one's responsibilities coming on again. But
work was the best cure. I immersed myself in a biography
of Hugh Lane and an edition of my *Kiltartan Poetry Book*. I
worked at my plays, writing down on scraps of paper the
dialogue I heard from tenants or neighbours. I never had
to travel far for my characters—they came to my door. I
had no ambition as a playwright when we started the
theatre movement, but when I saw that all the best plays
were serious, I felt there was a need for comedy to lighten
the load—audiences love comedy—so I set out to supply it.
When we played them in London, one Friday night the
applause and cries of 'Author' went on till I had to come
on to the stage, and I was cheered just as I had been in
Dublin. I could have made money from my plays if I had
permitted them to be performed in England and America.
I had offers and I was vexed with Yeats for objecting for I
needed the money. But then I changed my mind. I saw it
would weaken our own theatre if my plays were taken from

it and made common elsewhere. Besides, there was no controversy surrounding them, and Yeats and I were at our best when we had a fight on our hands, and our most memorable moments at the Abbey were when we faced controversy. We took on Dublin Castle over Shaw's play *The Shewing Up of Blanco Posnet*, which the British censors had banned, and we won that battle. And we faced the wrath of the Nationalists when we produced Synge's masterpiece, *The Playboy of the Western World*. Now, I never really liked the play—there was far too much swearing in it—but I was prepared to fight for it, especially when they accused us of bringing the Irish character into disrepute. Later, I travelled with the play to America and faced riots for a second time. On the opening night in New York, eggs, potatoes, watches, rosaries and smell bombs were hurled on to the stage. Anything that wasn't nailed down was thrown at the actors. And in Philadelphia, a lady was heard to ask her companion, 'And what do you really think of Lady Gregory's play—*The Cowboy of the Western World?*'

It was in America that I again made the acquaintance of John Quinn, the lawyer and philanthropist. We had met when he visited Coole some years earlier and now he proved a worthy ally as we defended *The Playboy* against the militants. I stayed in his apartment in New York for a brief period, and although he was younger than I was, I became infatuated with him. When I returned to Ireland I wrote to him—'My John, my dear John, my own John, not other people's John, I love you, I care for you, I believe in you. Oh my darling, am I not lonely after you? Why do I love you so much?' He replied, 'I often think of you over there with the grandchildren.'

But of all the disputes we faced at the Abbey, I was especially proud of the stand we took over O'Casey's *The Plough and the Stars* and Yeats's rousing riposte to the rioters:

> 'You have disgraced yourselves again. Is this going to be a recurring celebration of Irish genius? Synge first, now O'Casey! Dublin has again rocked the cradle of a reputation. From such a theatre as this went forth the fame of Synge. Equally, tonight, the fame of O'Casey is born. This is his apotheosis!'

O'Casey, listening in the wings, was pleased, if a little puzzled, for he had to wait until he got home to look up 'apotheosis' in the dictionary. *The Plough and the Stars* is an overpowering play. I felt at the end of it as if I should never care to look at another. Those quarrelling, drinking women have such tenderness and courage, as have the men. It's a wonderful play.

Life outside the Abbey during all this time was no less eventful. During the Rising, I was at my home and cut off completely from news of what was happening in Dublin. We were in the centre of a disturbed district, and with rails pulled up at one side and roads barricaded on the other, we were absolutely without news of anything. At an early opportunity, I went up to the Abbey and heard that the actors had been gathering for the matinee on Easter Monday when they heard shots and realised by degrees what was going on. The Abbey building itself escaped by a miracle; bricks from burning buildings fell even on the steps. The whole place was filled with smoke and dust. Everyone had a story to tell. In St. Stephen's Green, the rebels were shooting from the roof of a house. The lady it belonged to said she didn't like this, and they said it was all right—if the soldiers came she could go down to the cellar and be safe. But she said it was the noise she didn't like and so they moved off to another roof. One night, as I was leaving the Abbey, I walked into an ambush. My companions flung themselves to the ground but far from following their example, I drew myself up to my full height and I shouted, 'Up the Rebels!'

During the Civil War, I feared for the survival of Coole when so many of the big houses, like Roxborough, had been commandeered. My nephew and his wife had seen it coming and were packing and hiding away the valuables when the raiders arrived with a paper saying that since the house belonged to a Freemason and a Protestant, it must be given up to shelter Belfast refugees. The refugees never arrived but the house was maliciously burned to the ground. It pained me to see my family home in ruins. And it wasn't only the grand homes that were attacked. Going to church, I saw a cloud of smoke over Gort where the barracks had been burned, the walls alone left standing. The Gort people were so angry because if the wind had been in a bad quarter, the whole town would have burned down.

Friends urged me to fly my house but I refused. 'Through thirty years of widowed life,' I told them, 'Coole has been my home. I have cared for the parkland, planted trees; indeed the royalties from all my books grew into trees. I have lived here and I will die here and no one will force me to leave.' When one of my tenants threatened me with violence, I showed him how easy it would be to shoot me through the unshuttered window of this room. I told him

that nightly from six to seven I sit at this table, the blinds
drawn up.

A few years ago, I had an operation for cancer. I went up
to Dublin on a Friday. A lump had developed a week or so
ago in my breast. And though I was determined not to
have anything done that would keep me from home while
the holidays lasted, I went to see Dr. Slattery, and he said it
must come out, the sooner the better. And the next
morning, at a quarter to eleven, I was laid on the table, no
chloroform, just a local anaesthetic—it lasted about twenty
minutes.

I hadn't much pain, though feeling the knife working
about made me feel queer. So I fixed my mind upon a
river, the river at Roxborough, imagined it as it flowed
from the mountains through the flat land from
Kilchreest—under the road bridge, then under the
Volunteer Memorial bridge; through the deer park, then
deepened; salleys and bulrushes on one side, where coots
and wild fowl make their nests—on the other, the green
lawns; past the house, past the long line of buildings, the
stables, the kennels, the dairy, the garden walls; then,
narrow and deep, it turned the old mill wheel supplying
water for the steam engine that made the saw mills work.
Then the division, the parting of the waters, the otter's
cave, the bed of soft mud; the dip of the stream
underground, rising later to join its sunlit branch; a
rushing current again, past Ravahasey, Caherlinney, Poll
Na Sionnach, Esserkelly, Castleboy; bridges again and then
through thickets of laurel, beside a forsaken garden—a
sting of pain here from the knife, but I only made a face
and heard a voice say, 'Put in another drop'—and then by

a sloping field of daffodils—and so at last to the high road where it left our demesne.

Some pain again. And for a moment I thought of that river that bounded my second phase of life, rising in the park at Coole, flowing under the high poplars on its steep bank, vanishing under rocks that nature has made a bridge; then flowing on again till it widened into the lake. But before I had come to its disappearance under the rocks at Inchy, the Surgeon told me the knife had done its work. I was praised for courage and told I was 'very good'.

With Robert's death, the estate passed to Margaret. She held on to it for a time and then she said she couldn't afford to keep it, and despite my resistance, she decided to sell it to the Forestry Department. It was better so. The days of landed property have passed, but I continue to live in the big, old draughty house, paying rent—something of a come down for a Persse!

Last night in the library, the firelight, the lamplight shining on the rich bindings of that wall of books, and this evening, down by the lake, so silent, beautiful, Crannagh so peaceful—'the tilled, familiar land'—and later as I looked from my window at the sunset beyond the blue range of hills, I felt so grateful, as I have done often of late, to my husband who brought me to this house and home.

As I've said, at my time of life I should be content to sit still and meditate. I have painful arthritis now and I'm getting increasingly deaf. Sometimes the pains are very hard to bear. But what can one do? Such a waste of time when I can't write. Yeats visits me often, such a mercy—though I hide my suffering from him as far as I can. There are some that think I made a tin god of him but that is not so—I saw his genius and I provided a sanctuary where that genius might flourish. I approved his marriage, and I watched with pride as he and his bride, and later their two splendid children, settled in Ballylee. He gave me so much more than I ever gave him, and I'm grateful for that.

I have travelled far, very far; there are few who have travelled as far as I have, and there are few who would not make me welcome at their hearth. Sometimes my feet are tired and my hands are tired, but there is no quiet in my heart. Oh, pain! I'll try to get a little sleep on the sofa, bye and bye.

She exits

Blackout

Postscript

Lady Gregory died peacefully at her home in Coole Park on 23rd May 1932. A few days earlier, despite crippling arthritis, she walked round all the rooms in the big house as if to say goodbye to the place that had given her so much joy. W.B. Yeats had remained with her most of the previous year but he was in Dublin on business when news of her final illness reached him. He set out for Coole immediately, but on his arrival at Gort, he was met with the news that Lady Gregory had died in the night. Her daughter-in-law, Margaret, and two of the grandchildren, Anne and Catherine, had been at her bedside; her grandson, Richard, was in England sitting his final examinations for the Royal Engineers.

Lady Gregory was buried, at her own request, in a simple oak coffin in the New Cemetery in Galway, beside her sister Arabella; the mausoleum at Kiltartan, where Sir William had been buried, having been sealed years earlier. Three months later, the entire contents of Coole were sold at auction. The house remained empty until the early 1940s, when it was demolished and the stone used by a local contractor for building projects in Gort. Today, the estate is a National Nature Reserve. In 1992, an Interpretative Centre was opened. The garden with its autograph tree on the great lawn has been preserved, and visitors may see the stables and the footprint of the house—all that remains of the building that played such a vital role in the Irish Renaissance.

Lady Gregory was the last of the Gregorys to live at Coole. In 1927, the estate was sold by Margaret to the Forestry Department, and a year later, she married Captain Guy Gough of Lough Cutra, the estate adjacent to Coole. Ironically, Lough Cutra had been the scene of the dinner party at which the young Augusta Persse, according to her later recollections, had been 'too shy to ask for the salt and had a thoroughly unappetising meal.' Margaret and her husband lived at Celbridge Abbey, home of Hester Van Homrigh, Jonathan Swift's 'Vanessa', and then at Leixlip Castle, County Kildare. They also had a house in Chelsea. The children, Richard, Anne and Catherine, lived with them but sought opportunities to return to Coole to stay with Grandma, especially during the holidays. Richard attended Harrow and Cambridge before joining the Royal Engineers, and after marriage, all three grandchildren settled in England.

Regarding the Hugh Lane collection of Impressionist pictures, the subject of the disputed 1915 codicil—Lady Gregory persisted throughout her lifetime in her efforts to have them returned to Dublin from the National Gallery in London, but to no avail. In 1959, an agreement was reached between the British and Irish governments by which the pictures were divided into two groups, alternately housed in the two capitals.